Jesus Ascends
AND OTHER BIBLE STORIES

BY REBECCA GLASER

ILLUSTRATED BY BILL FERENC AND EMMA TRITHART

SPARK HOUSE FAMILY

MINNEAPOLIS

Contents

25 24 23 22 21 20 19 18 17 16   1 2 3 4 5 6 7 8 9 10

Book design by Toolbox Studios, Dave Wheeler, Alisha Lofgren, Janelle Markgren,
  and Ivy Palmer Skrade
Colorization: Dave Wheeler

Library of Congress Cataloging-in-Publication Data

Glaser, Rebecca Stromstad.
  Jesus ascends and other Bible stories / by Rebecca Glaser ; illustrated
by Bill Ferenc and Emma Trithart.
      pages cm. — (Holy Moly Bible storybooks)
  ISBN 978-1-5064-0254-3 (alk. paper)
1. Jesus Christ—Resurrection—Juvenile literature. 2. Bible stories,
English—Gospels. I. Ferenc, Bill, illustrator. II. Title.
  BT482.G53 2016
  232.9'7--dc23
                            2015026223
Printed on acid-free paper

Printed in China

V63474; 9781506402543; FEB2016

Thomas Believes

The disciples were sad and afraid. Jesus had died, and they were worried they might be in trouble for being his disciples. They hid in a locked room. All of them were there, except Thomas.

3

"Peace be with you," Jesus said. He showed his disciples the wounds in his hands and side. The disciples' mouths hung open. It was really Jesus! Alive again!

Circle the wounds in Jesus' hands.

One week later, ALL the disciples hid in the locked room, including Thomas. Jesus appeared again!

"Peace be with you," Jesus said. Thomas saw the wounds in Jesus' hands and side. "Jesus, it's really you!" he exclaimed.

"You believe because you have seen," Jesus said. "Blessed are those who believe without seeing."

Breakfast with Jesus

Some of the disciples fished all night but didn't catch anything! By morning, their bellies were as empty as their nets. And it was time for breakfast!

9

As the sun rose, the disciples heard a voice from the shore: "You haven't caught any fish, have you?"

"Not one all night!" they called back.

"Throw your nets out again on the other side of the boat!" the voice told them.

With a gentle swoosh, they dropped their nets in the water one more time. Immediately, fish came swimming and splashing and jumping into the nets!

There were so many fish, the disciples could barely lift them! With a heave and a grunt, they pulled the fish into the boat. Not just ten fish or twenty, but 153!

Draw some fish leaping toward the boat.

As flopping fish filled the boat, the disciples realized the voice belonged to Jesus! They paddled back to shore.

Jesus sat by a small fire, toasting bread and fish for breakfast. He shared with the exhausted fishermen. The disciples munched their breakfast, filled with awe that Jesus was alive again.

The Road to Emmaus

After Jesus died, Cleopas and his friend were walking along the road to Emmaus. They talked about how Jesus had died, and they wondered if he was really alive again.

As they walked, another man joined them. "What's wrong?" the stranger asked them.

"Have you not heard about Jesus?" they replied.

"He was crucified and died," Cleopas and his friend told the stranger. "But this morning, some of his followers say they saw Jesus alive!"

"Didn't the prophets say that God's Son would die and rise again?" the stranger asked.

As evening came, Cleopas and his friend invited the stranger to stay at their house. They went inside to eat. The man broke the bread, blessed it, and gave it to them.

Suddenly, they realized this stranger was Jesus! He really was alive again!

The Great Call

The disciples were filled with hope. Mary Magdalene had seen Jesus—alive! She told them Jesus wanted to meet them in Galilee, so they hurried off to see him.

Up high on a mountain peak in Galilee, Jesus appeared to the disciples. They rejoiced to see their friend and worshipped him.

Then Jesus spoke. "You have faithfully followed me, but now it's your turn. I am giving you the authority to teach and baptize in my name."

Color the woman being baptized.

"Travel near and far. Tell people about me! Baptize them in the name of the Father, Son, and Holy Spirit."

"Spread the good news of God's love. Make disciples, and teach them to obey my commandments. I will always be with you."

23

The disciples traveled near and far.
They shared the good news of
God's love and made disciples in
nations everywhere.

Jesus Ascends

The disciples whispered in hushed voices. "Jesus died!" one said. "Can he really be alive again?"

"But Mary and her friend saw him," another added. "Maybe it IS true!"

"Peace be with you," Jesus said.

It SOUNDED like Jesus. The disciples peeked out from their hiding places. It LOOKED like Jesus. "Why are you afraid?" Jesus said. "I'm not a ghost. Please bring me something to eat."

27

The disciples gave Jesus a broiled fish.
With a bite and a swallow, he ate it right up.
Everyone was amazed—ghosts can't eat!
It really WAS Jesus!

Jesus told them, "Everything the prophets wrote has come true. I died, but now I am alive again! You have seen it, and you believe!"

The disciples followed Jesus as he climbed up a hill near Bethany. As Jesus blessed them, he was carried up to heaven.

The disciples worshipped Jesus and were filled with great joy. It was the last time they would see Jesus. But they were excited to share the good news of God's love with everyone!

More Activities

LOOK AND FIND

Find the in Thomas Believes on pages 3–8.

After Jesus died, the disciples were afraid that people would come after them too, so they hid behind a locked door. How did Jesus get in?

Find the  in the Breakfast with Jesus story on pages 9–14.

First the disciples tried and tried, but they caught no fish. When they listened to Jesus, their nets were full of fish!

Find the  in The Road to Emmaus on pages 15–18.

The two people didn't recognize Jesus until he blessed and broke the bread like he did with the disciples at the Last Supper.

Find the in The Great Call on pages 19–24.

Jesus told the disciples to teach, heal, and baptize people all around the world in the name of the Father, the Son, and the Holy Spirit.

Find the  in the Jesus Ascends story on pages 25–30.

Jesus ate fish in front of the disciples to show them he had a real body and wasn't a ghost or a vision.

ACTION PRAYER

Open your eyes! *(point to your eyes)*

Jesus is here!

We can see Jesus' love in our smiles. *(point to mouth and smile)*

We can feel Jesus' love in our hands. *(clap your hands)*

We can feel Jesus' love in our feet. *(stomp your feet)*

We can feel Jesus' love in our hearts. *(pat your chest)*

We can feel Jesus' love all over. *(wiggle all over)*

Open your eyes! *(point to your eyes)*

Jesus is here!

Amen.

MATCHING GAME

Match the person from the Bible with the fact about them.

1. I didn't believe the other disciples when they first told me Jesus was alive.

2. After I appeared to the disciples for the last time, I ascended into heaven.

3. We thought Jesus was a stranger when he first started walking with us.

4. We ate fish for breakfast with Jesus.

Barnyard Buddies

In the Buffalo Pasture

by Patricia M. Stockland
illustrated by Todd Ouren

Special thanks to content consultant:
James S. Cullor, DVM, PhD

magic
Wagon

visit us at www.abdopublishing.com

Published by Magic Wagon, a division of the ABDO Group, 8000 West 78th Street, Edina, Minnesota 55439. Copyright © 2010 by Abdo Consulting Group, Inc. International copyrights reserved in all countries. All rights reserved. No part of this book may be reproduced in any form without written permission from the publisher.

Looking Glass Library™ is a trademark and logo of Magic Wagon.

Printed in the United States.

 Manufactured with paper containing at least 10% post-consumer waste

Text by Patricia M. Stockland
Illustrations by Todd Ouren
Edited by Amy Van Zee
Interior layout and design by Becky Daum
Cover design by Becky Daum

Library of Congress Cataloging-in-Publication Data
Stockland, Patricia M.
  In the buffalo pasture / by Patricia M. Stockland ; illustrated by Todd Ouren.
      p. cm. — (Barnyard buddies)
  Includes index.
  ISBN 978-1-60270-641-5
  1. American bison—Juvenile literature. I. Ouren, Todd. ill. II. Title.
  SF401.A45S74 2010
  636.2'92—dc22
                          2009007484

The spring morning is warm. The cow looks over the pasture. **Moo, moo.**

Adult female buffalo are called cows.
Buffalo live in pastures and on plains.

The cow has a new calf. The calf
can already stand.

Baby buffalo are called calves. They can stand
and run just a few hours after they are born.

The new calf is hungry. It nudges its mother for milk.

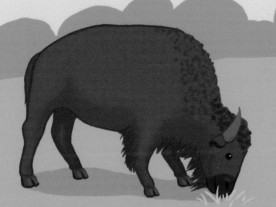

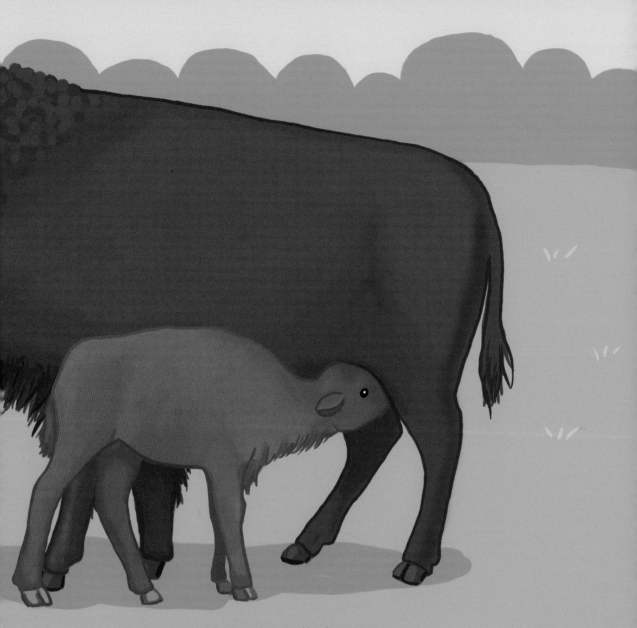

A calf drinks milk from its
mother for about six months.

The cow and calf are part of a herd. The herd grazes together in the big pasture.

Buffalo herds need a lot of space to graze. Buffalo
eat grass, wild hay, and other prairie plants.

The calf follows its mother in the pasture.
The herd watches for predators while it eats.

Sometimes wolves and grizzly bears prey on young calves. Cows are very protective of their young.

As the summer goes on, the calf grows bigger.
It learns to graze with the herd. Its fur gets thick.

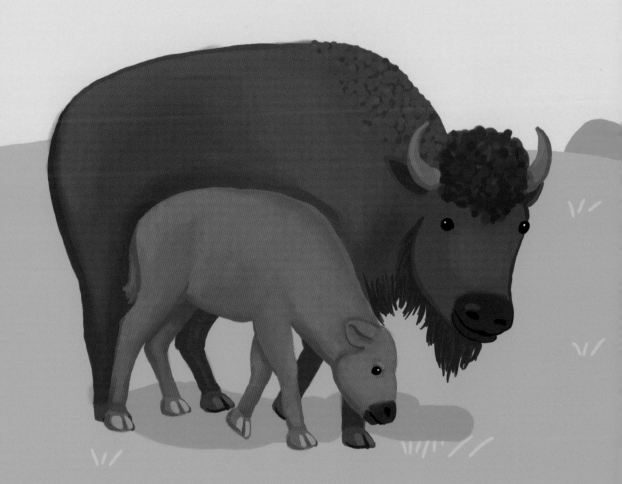

Buffalo have thick coats of soft wool and coarse hair.

The calf has grown large. It no longer needs its mother. The rancher weans the calf.

A calf is weaned when it has been
separated from its mother.

15

The weather grows colder. The rancher takes some of the herd to market.

Ranchers raise buffalo for meat and hides.

The other buffalo in the herd spend the winter outside. The rancher gives the herd extra hay to eat.

Buffalo have thick coats to keep
them warm and dry in cold and
snowy weather.

In the spring, the pasture becomes green again. New calves arrive. **Moo, moo!**

21

Buffalo Diagram

ear

hump

horn

tail

eye

mouth

hoof

Glossary

graze—to feed on land covered by grass.
hide—the skin of an animal.
market—where animals are bought and sold.
pasture—land covered with grass that animals can eat.
predator—an animal that hunts other animals.
rancher—a person who raises, cares for, and sells
    range animals, such as buffalo, cattle, and horses.

Fun Facts

 The actual name for North American buffalo is American bison. But, most people call them buffalo!

 Ranchers raise buffalo, but buffalo are not domesticated animals. This means they do not naturally live with or near humans.

 Buffalo can live to be 25 years old.

 Adult male buffalo are called bulls.

 Sometimes buffalo burp up food from the stomach and chew it again. This helps buffalo digest food.

 Newborn buffalo calves weigh about 45 pounds (20 kg). An adult bull can weigh 2,000 pounds (900 kg) or more. That is about as much as a car!

 All adult buffalo have horns.

 Buffalo make many sounds, including grunts, bellows, and moos.

 Even though they are big, buffalo are very fast. They can run at speeds of 40 miles per hour (64 kph).

Index